Party Games

Written by Tom Pipher and Bob Eschenbach
Illustrated by Kerry Gemmill

Pablo and Paul are best friends.
They go to school together.
They play together.

Sometimes they play at Pablo's house.
Pablo's mother gives them milk and tacos.
Sometimes they play at Paul's house.
Paul's mother gives them milk and sandwiches.

One day, Paul asks Pablo,
"Can you come to my birthday party?
We'll have fun and games.
We'll have cake and ice cream."

Pablo goes to Paul's birthday party.
Paul shows Pablo a fun game –
Pin the Tail on the Donkey.
Paul gives a tail to Pablo.
Paul puts a blindfold on Pablo.
Paul spins Pablo around
and around and around.
Pablo must go to the donkey
and pin on a tail.

Other children also pin on tails.
Amanda pins a tail
on the donkey's nose.
All the children laugh.
Juan pins a tail
on the donkey's leg.
All the children laugh.

Pablo has pinned a tail on the right spot.
Pablo is the winner.
All the children get prizes.

Pablo goes home.
He tells his mother,
"We had cake and ice cream.
We played Pin the Tail on the Donkey.
I pinned the tail on the right spot
on the donkey."
Pablo tells his mother,
"The donkey game was fun.
Paul is my best friend."

Pablo's birthday is coming soon.
Pablo asks Paul,
"Can you come to my birthday party?
We'll have fun and games.
We'll have cake and ice cream."

Paul goes to Pablo's party.
Pablo's mother knows
just the game to play.
She hangs a *burro piñata* in a tree.
It is full of lollies.

Pablo shows Paul a fun game –
Break the *Piñata*.
Pablo gives a stick to Paul.
Pablo puts a blindfold on Paul.
Pablo spins Paul around
and around and around.
Paul must swing at the *piñata*
and break it.

Other children also take swings.
Amanda swings at the *piñata*
and misses three times.
All the children laugh.
Juan swings at the *piñata*
and misses three times.
All the children laugh.

Paul swings at the *piñata* again and breaks it.
All the lollies fall to the ground.

All the children fall on each other.
They laugh and pick up the lollies.

Paul goes home.
He tells his mother,
"We had cake and ice cream.
We played Break the *Piñata*.
I broke the donkey *piñata*."
Paul tells his mother,
"The *piñata* game was fun.
I love the *piñata* game.
Pablo is my best friend."